AND THEN IT COMES BLOWING

poetic expressions of

George E Harris

Published by William Cornelius Harris Publishing

In collaboration

with

London Poetry Books

Supporting Mental Health in Performing Arts

ISBN 978-1-911232-13-1

c/o Open Door, 224 Jamaica Road, London SE16

W
C
H
P

info@londonpoetrybooks.com

www.londonpoetrybooks.com

To those people I value, to those I admire and those that inspire.

My partner in love and creative output Alison O'Melia.

To my friend and poet Jerry Hope who was and is an inspiration.

To my family John, Nora and Simon, Emily and friends in Cornwall.

To the entire O'Melia family (too many to name!)

To all the people whom have helped in creating the sounds with me and Alison as Brother G and the Trouble - Walt Shaw, Mitzy Valentine, Agata Lisowska with Lorin Jasper Halsall and other folk in participation.

To the people whom have given us the opportunities to perform: Joe Duggan, Ken Champion / More Poetry, Dark Arts Circus, Paper Tiger, Artsmith Live and the Crystal Palace Overground Festival, Noreen Meehan and Andy Stem.

To Metamono – Jono, Mark and Paul plus Nick.

To all my artist friends Clives (x2!), Chris, Beth, Dave, Rob, Tracey, Corey, Nev, Sharyn,Vic, Mark and Claire, Paul, Anthony and many others.

The Protagonist! / Keith and Olivia

Candice Moule

The Dory Llama

Jeremy Corbyn

Jason Why / London Poetry Books for putting this publication out.

Further research into the works of George E Harris:

www.georgeharrisphoto.co.uk

www.worldofsurprises.co.uk

Contents

Black and white photographs throughout by George E Harris.

The following words can be spoken aloud, chanted or sung.
Some have been placed with music improvisations and some
just on their own.

PARADISE WALK

That smile as the street cleaner fed the pigeons,
taking scraps out of his trolley bin on the early morning.
Spreading them on the circle island, satisfied in his rebellion.

I nodded and smiled, seemed we had an understanding
through the sunshine beaming, between the mayhem of wings,
birds going crazy over the laid down morsels.

Months before, on and off I often saw this man,
Joe is his name,
angry at the lack of care on his patch.

The local businesses used to give him a coffee or two,
an exchange for clearing the surrounding streets,
now seems devoid in the divide and selfish enterprise.

Got me to thinking about our selfie nation
on this crumbling walk,
wake up our nightmares are arising right outside.

Wake up we have a task to deal,
against agendas to pit one against another,
people against people, worker vs worker and friend against friend.

Sub divided populous with futures uncertain.
Powers stamping on those in need,
a danger to us all within this broken challenge.

Its not a game show, quizzed to see whom comes out alive,
its real, very real, faced up
in this hyper reality of an elite offensive.

My mind now casts back to the island
going crazy for breadcrumbs,
who's paradise walk is it?

THE BIRD PEOPLE

A shift in the galaxy,
spatial plains wake up across the river bank
in observations of people having good times.

Umbrella holding girl
running down the hill in criss cross laughter,
heading to their stop.

On my way home, gentle breeze now
increasing droplets sprinkle the night,
this breeze explodes to imagined flight.

Motion forward and up,
almost,
take off.

On the edges of civilisation time was growing out of the diseased valleys,
to begin with window blinds and fans were stuck into flesh,
household implements being used to make flight.

After the great winds
came the days of melding, a worldwide epidemic,
people started to blend with their everyday objects and utilities.

Initially the roof ramp of Vauxhall stops
was used as a take-off runway,
now long gone are the bus routes and other clogged transport links.

The skies are full,
patterned in motion above the cities
come the bird people.

CONVERSING WITH A VOICE OVER

A shadow of a tree throwing bombs
co-ordinates South by South East.
Fitting bay in economic scandals,
the baron is back in system electric,
rhetoric through the mediators.

Skip to first place,
smash and grab raid in the balustrades,
quadraphonic mods in jubilee horizons.
Hype on its way
in those social broadcasts
through the stray rag and bone.

Cleaning the soul winding wheel,
simply put through a smile,
a conversation with voice over narrating through the forth wall.

Its in the air, what not,
ramifications in building blocks to migrating rivers,
these rails of fortune pound in a euphoric glide through the northern heart.

Early morning call outs through trumpet sounds,
up and down the winding streets, bring out your scrap,
your loose ends, dialogues to ringing, tears and joys in destination.

Memories of Reggae Bike Man,
sound system strapped to the handle bars
riding the streets all hours, up and down
bringing peace and a smile through the soul.

Migrating in the floating world,
antenna grids in universal embrace
at the barriers formations retraced in shuffles.
Between the runner and the walker a build on memory in integrated place,
homecomings, movements elsewhere, over, over and over,
someone's out there with a big spoon stirring.

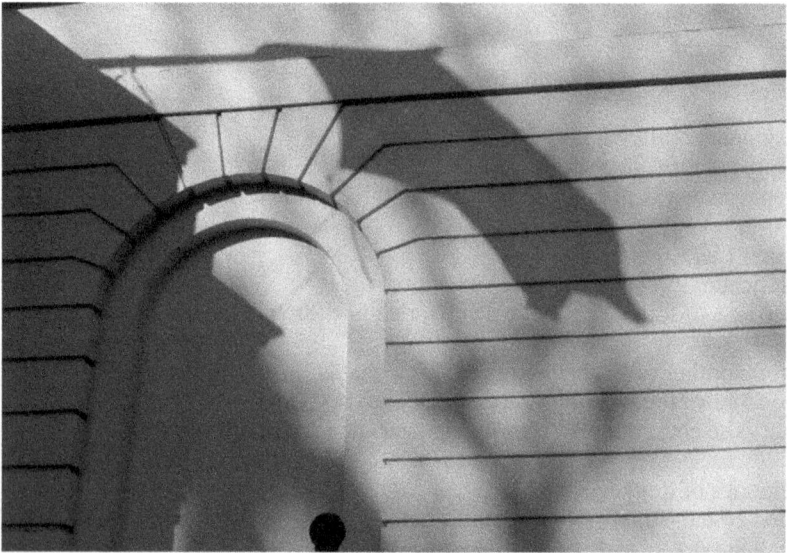

OPTIONAL FOCUS

Slipping in and out, this beauty at a glance,
the sleep service is provided at cut price.
Time is being run through at speed.

This rant at a slant, news events echos,
taking place in overlapping succession,
intervention set to confuse, divert invention, integrity is now a memory.

Tricks with fury and anger flowing.
This heat in the breathing blast furnace,
industry a heritage site punching to heights,
hired to lobby the next contestants on the way down.

Needs be reality, oh lets text the highlights
and treat it to some contempt. In opinion flows of optional focus,
a constant redressing in a plan to satisfy
every corner to hold in the terror, discipline and punish.

Measures to buy out the cracks and manipulate the fact
as the pleasure is ours in those suppressed optical illusions.
Perspectives in reality, it doesn't really exist,
swimming in the dead pool stillness.

Im floundering in this uncompromising journey of fractions,
in mind lights, time seems like HD Unreal.

A need to look at the succession maps of splatters,
paint markings, piss stains and vomit comets.
A certain ratio of grid triangulations
that tens of thousands more building in resistance, talking and taking action.

Chartered, fiscal, visceral and twisted contact, turnaround roundabouts.
Oh yeah, do ya, not on our lives, take it back.
It's like the domino effect, falling on this one triggers the next,
perpetual stop signs being driven through
upon a need to bring to task this current state.

BLOOD FLOW

Blowing in the distance
angelic voices in split shadow domains.
The last free house of the wilderness
sailing away on box's, cartons and newspaper bargains.

Here in the alpha city provinces,
hold on its here in distraction, blending in the neon dawn.
A contemplation of conscience and consequence,
hideous minds, you, yes you on the path to behold or explode.

Just another day on this commuted missed bus.
The winds rushing through channels of concrete spires
and trees bend in the shales of rain, sheets across the street.
This cinematic light swing on window panes,
trails of folks sweeping over crossover towers.

Two days ago riding out, monkey man, rush, panic, scream and pressure on.
11.45pm last night the cold is within her, all down on side of body crawl.
7.48am that morning the stand off
with the street cleaner and special brewed matador.
Blocked, beaten down and blood drawn, devoured in the observations.

As time grew in the chests of the city dwellers,
mapped out and hardwired clocks pass through the blood flow.
The triangles, bells ring out of residue soaked daily forecasts
and borderline feelings of hope in no shadows of doubt.

Determined walkers about turn and walk the other way.
We fall into this over and over,
look both ways and the other way round,
elevations in three minutes of heaven.

Only the faithful maintain the course of the cause.
In allegory to the represented,
definitions on the line with soul pounding divisions.
I want you baby, rise up and hold the rhyme.

IN THE TIC TOC

The old man walks,
timed precisely
with carry all on hand,
everyday in the early morning
towards the flats near my stop.

Last night the conversation delved
into our Sci-Fi world with things going so fast,
its outdated as soon as it hits the market.

The numbing effect of the day to day stops,
bring on the chants of the beautiful fog,
take it forward in your stillness of open possibility.

The digging takes place in the city boroughs,
 planned or just goes ahead without an after thought,
underground lairs of the wealthy,
unseen in subterranean grooming.

Flipped and reliving,
Wells time machine in
advanced Victorian engineering
and 21st Century technological
knowing of the fourth wall,
bitten through and advancing into the 6th dimension.

Missing letters of verse, those that I never wrote,
the winding spine, triumphs in the tic toc,
pastures of utopia in my constant waking
and sleep inside this crust,
cemented in the consciousness.

I'm the spirit in and out ghostlike on the margins,
partially dissolved fruit in the still pool
champions of contracted diversion
on a morning ride to prop up higher gains.
Co-operate you need to speak it out,
remember as well as write it down.

Hooded mirrored faced sentinels,
guardians on this morning ride, side by side,
criss-cross slides shifting the auto-plane.

Drifting in with dreaded feelings under the soft sunrise.
Those electric sounds now floating behind,
reading and encapsulating the no rhythm and non reason.

This wake up call of
governmental street peddlers,
upper this and lower that,
ripping the human rights from under us.

Dismayed with policy and lack of full understanding.
The apathy is the killer, but can be the energy.
Now on a path to hold with account and take the sight.

NO POOR DOORS

Droplets in patterns singing
to inner city planning,
an inner flux of super haven.

No poor doors (we sing).

Demolition dust hangs in the air,
un-fractured drift
on planetary mission to the outer rings.

We shout out to the no poor doors.

With atoms cracking,
the satellites rapidly building.
Taking homes on the run
on a mass movement out of the inner city.

The beat comes fast in the chants of no poor doors.

Twisted in lightening community walls.
This line up disappearing.
The road to dropout observations.
NO just shut it, I'm just sitting here
and speaking about the no poor doors.

Now in the outer regions on high
the lines of trees in plantations
set around mining and working the land properties.
History redefined within its wooded tranquility.

Then and now, countryside to urban definitions.
Hiding the real reasons of whats not seen and isn't really there.
News deflects the truth in separating
and hushes the mass.

We have to sing out to the no poor doors.

Capability Brown in the 1700s,
a sorcerer of garden viewpoint and perspectives.
Flooded villages to gain a good view for the landed gentry.

No poor doors to those in history and
that of the current social housing in jeopardy.
It seems the spirits of capability lives on.

Housing trusts, can we?
Land banking in the spread
and rise of the new horizon lines.

Now in the shadows of the blacked out tower.
A programme is in place to rehouse those whom have lost their homes,
possessions, family and friends, within the empty glass spires and avenues.

It has brought to light a social division in attitudes within a society.
Vast wealth with a hidden and extreme poverty holding just there.

In this light people are saying not on my doorstep,
I've paid for this air of luxury.
Abominable 21st Victorian attitudes hiding
from the depths of the human disaster.

This tower left to rot and cutting corners, failed council checks and policy.
Blood on their hands, truths coming undone in the days of horror.
Dominoes spreading countrywide.

We say No and we say No again
and so then we say Yes to opening the doors,
open them wide to all whom have nowhere.

BLANKETS

In the fabrication of stories lost,
the lifting or a sense of freedom in the air,
but little scares bring it offers on the transcendent road.

Luminous blue lines,
splatters of blue blood
on the bus seats just forward of me.

Listings of the hours lost as the clocks strike backwards.

Comprehension of time fractioned
in habitual mesh of gas tower reboots.

Imprinted stamps,
those woodcuts on corner shop facades.

The dust has been falling,
the future is now here.
Blanket gardens are desert beige
under a haze hanging in particle splinters.

Praying for a breeze and changes in this silent storm,
sand like petroleum smell hanging so close,
thin air drop in poisonous smash.

Seems like an unstoppable machine.

Its now the weekend
and the lifting is here again
with park bird feeders in freedom flow,
now well under offer in the dance of crows.

WIND IN SILENCE

Rushing the leaves,
heads reaching on limit,
primed status to ancient testing while you wait.

Hit on crisis point,
the heads on overload
going into hyperdrive.

Its in my nature to worry,
scared to think of
what is happening over the road and the other seas.

Hold up our values in feeding seeds.
We need to be on the right side of history
and not let things just happen
because its somehow nothing to do with us.

We do have a say, we all do.
I'm not sitting back and letting it happen.
We have to take that stand and rise up
and not hold that wind in silence.

THE GROWL

Hound deals and hand shakes,
the growl of the earth preserved
in salt over ground to bridges,
plagues of withering shapes,
figures in mist soaked streets.

Its gone that far, blu blu bla bla blap in succession rap.
Imitating gun shots, he says
'today five pound I get that five pounds'
holding the passport, receipts in hand, in the face in the rounds.
Smoked identity in fear stops, hear creeps
in translation steps of journey truths
and songs for someone missing.

Haunted bus stop moments
I could take another route,
why not, what the hell...
I have to get there on time at least
five minutes before start time.

Ten hours down, two to go, hallucinating in repeated values.
Idealism is now an after thought,
human machinery to fashion excess.
Up and down, called to collect / bring.
In effectual in a name posing to non elective sources
playing the machinery in hunted game.

My growls of thought in succession rap,
fraught to the bone with spills on silence
caged up controlled by the bag phone.
What's the use I'm now a drone to this excess.
Operations resume after the ringing stops
on my way home, residue sharps and zombie pile
falling into mechanical trials.

WE GO KNOCKING

Its now on the doors, pounding those streets,
gaining information, talking and listening.

This amazing collective of individuals
campaigning on the trail highlight,
we go knocking.

Its our heart beat, passions and rage,
waking to those signs of no hope,
still we go knocking.

Gasping screaming in the breath
my monkey man is coming
in this early morning anxiety.
We Go Knocking.

The Turn is on,
lets bypass the media manipulations,
carry some hopes,
a huge turn out in the circle building.
We Go Knocking.

Convincing those
programmed to un-think that it is
strong, stable and just ok for their needs.
We Go Knocking.

The many not just the few
have time to clear obstructions
and disobey, just factor the decisions.
We Go Knocking.

To inspire like any struggle,
to think in the underlying soul,
meeting the drive home and beyond.
We Go Knocking.

ITS A DELIGHT TO HOLD YOU

Making tracks back home,
diverted through the concrete hole.
With prayers being sung so loud
and in the dead end 3- 4 people maybe more.
Sitting and talking outside an open door, setting the world to rights.

I reverse back, though listening,
making note of those that pass.
On the hill channel from city to village green
arriving on the day they celebrate the days of steam.
Dancers waiting on the edges to parading down the main streets

Those engineers of truth,
those engineers of hopes,
these engineers of empty space.

Tributes to a long gone episode of lets find the watery grave
with poems of electrical impulse and delayed conversations.
Inside the web of troubled mountains and unheard beats.

Its a delight to hold you as the rain pours through those songs.

Streams in the brain
in the spirit of the Capitols Cool Jerk.
Taking Actions on the waking street,
smoke shuffles of domino feet.
Increased resolve amongst the family nets.

Nuclear heat on border controls.
Carrier pigeons now taking notes over
broken telegraph wires and intersected rusting cables.
As we venture through the underground
it becomes increasingly obvious
that the wish lists and facing time has impacted into nothing.

Except its a delight to hold you as the brass bass hits.

CITY AM I

Concerns were raised with May-festoon alarm,
the people are at risk in restrictive policy making.
Regulation intimidation, brought possibles unbound,
un-costed meal stealers, old folks taxed in care onslaught,
means testing and foxes on the run.

Not for the city am I.

People of all, previously losing faith with a system.
Youth in grime now just regaining enthusiasms,
needing a real change and registering for the hope.
Oh city am I
the U-turns twists and on the bend.
Campaigns building in heights, now Whaaamm,
a reality hits in bloody tragedy and people have suffered, killed in a night.

This city am I, hash-tagged for a room, coming out,
taking a stand with those looking for their lost.
Praise these hearts moving way beyond in acts of kindness and selflessness.
Finding a place, shelter and the care in the world of the untempered extremes.

Instance in grief for a people cried,
outpourings on the social media searches and missing branches.
Oh come the City am I now calling it anything else
or putting blame is just not the way.
We need to overcome after this day and the next
to become much much more.
In truth we hold, never be played or be divided,
but come united in those facts for all.

DELIVERY OF THE CIRCUS OF FLIES

Closing my eyes and listen
to the sounds, those blips on the bus.
Then it says hello in a slow drifting voice.

Urgency of feeling now
that communication is cut,
physically channelling the anxiety,
as it comes to entertaining of what could be.

Speaking of which, I have no ideas as such
with the announcement life is on a one way image.

Crisis is here, taking on an unsettling edge.
Though winners today are upholding
in the recognition stakes.

With the trial of that,
its a bonus in circular sores
on painted shadows that
decorate a wooden white fence.

Now taking orders from an outstanding performance
in social obligations and on screen attacks.

We are now receiving a delivery of the circus of flies.

IN THE DOT DOT DOT

From the dust to acrylic,
above the smoke on hillside fogs.
Request stops, medicine rising,
this weekly stand off upon this daily route.

My soul is in the dot dot dot.

Out of the shadows in shots from the hip.
Cross purpose from the verse.
This voice translates the dawn
in daily dues to the dub inspector.

De costa studios, it will,
waiting here for a few minutes to change drivers.
Sounds like thunder above, squalls on the way.

This verse that borders in the unconscious zones,
those trails of frequent screams.
Now the burbling downstairs increases.

Witness upon the cauldron,
carriage goes at it.
New risings in the dot dot dot.

TRANSISTOR SALVATIONS

Internal workings of experience
amassed inside a warehouse, situated east-side.
Soaked streets mindset of transistor salvations.

Coming together once in a blue moon
the shifting voices collide in and out of electrical jet streams.
Circular saw blades hung in reverberation energy arising.

Murmurs in the maelstrom
holding the elevated cries of all.

Wondering minstrels slide through whispering dancers.
Then on to the other side a screen projects
a scene in timed quarterly motions of distorted heads.

Horn blasts and shadows burn bass note on words spoken.
Metal Screams through personal overlapped streams
in the instance of a movement.

True freedom through a graphic score upon twisting the sonic shells.
Enacted around and through the audience.
Welcoming in the beautiful cacophony, flipping the wires on the system.

BRIXTON BUS

View from this bus taken in a photograph
a day or two before
we are now remembering many faces, but just one soul.

Staring out on this starry sprawl,
inside the condensation filled top deck,
lights blurred covering the spoils of the days gone.

The wardrobe has split and the capsule is flying,
all the asteroids are now drawn in,
but the impossible is everything.

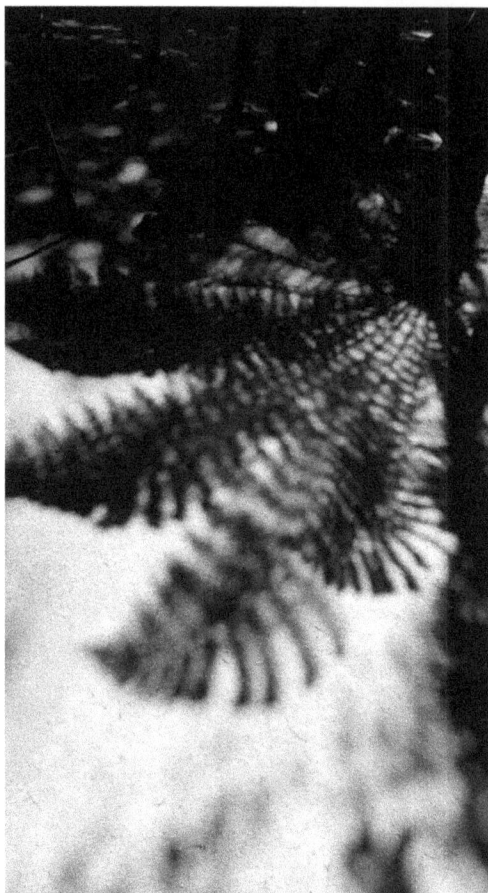

CROFT LAND

There's a feeling
I might be related
to a famous poet.
My father thinks that's a great possibility.

Those remaining truths in afterglow
on Cornish soil set in lucid views.
Transversing the place
and states of growing up.

In the elements on a brief, but now extended break.

Weather conditions in a to and throe position.
Quiet please the reports are coming again.
Blowing through whistling masts.

Rattle in the gamelan chant.
Beeble, bramble, gorse, brook and over again.
Beeble, bramble, gorse, brook and over again.
Beeble, bramble, gorse, brook and over again.

Lower, middle and top field dens,
formal gardens, croft land, swamp.
Ghosts to play a merry, merry memory dance.

In the celebration of
Beeble, bramble, gorse, brook and over again.
Beeble, bramble, gorse, brook and over again.
Beeble, bramble, gorse, brook and over again.

THE ROOM

Inside, listening to the planes fly by.
She's at peace with the sound.
Watching bouncing cables through the bedroom blinds.

Lying inside listening to the planes fly by,
recollecting themes on the hill.

Honorable trails in the disorder,
mutual and capital free.

UP IN THE THICKET

(photograph in excavated memory)

This reminds me of your death.
Particularly the long stare, prior to,
in thousand yards behind my head.

Introduced image in several years that depicts grey desert climb.

Eyes pin point in jaundiced yellow rising heat above
the five detectives of the apocalypse.

They in Victorian dress stand and stare, observational and statuesque.

Investigating shadow light and pastel shade,
squinting into the horizon.
Angels riding the dune express.

(in subsequence)

Post haste I walk,
need some time to think
and find a voice.

Spotted an image on a sign post outside St Martin in the Fields:
'missing person full details in height, eyes, hair,
weight, character traits and habits'.

In the centre I got to thinking over coffee
about the thousands of tourist photographs
that must have picked you up.

The all encompassing image of disappearance
fly posted in search of saviors passing.
Pigeon thieves on the prowl,
transferring instinct into impact and vice versa.
The cafe owner claps and its gone.

In succession the Trafalgar water flow speaking within soundings and hums.

Now at bus stop a left hand merc pulls up on Whitehall.
Fat tanned man with pin stripped suit gets out,
stares at me, briefcase in hand and scuttles into a door nearby.

In this destination south seemingly unconnected moments
reflect the greater defectors of the case.

Introductions took place near the metropolitan drinking fountain
and later on watching the skeletal dancers in Max Roach Park.
Now conversations resume the unspoken bonds.

(in prequel)

Across the square I walk,
passing a crowd bunched upon the steps.
Just huddled under umbrellas to the strain of bagpipes played.
Seemed to be a moment of giving some respect
in mourning and or a Scottish surrealists club in hats.

I liked to think both.

As it stood all reports came in three
leading to a full heritage up in the thicket.

Investigation central now undertakes
printing and publications as a sideline
in graphic novels and verse.

I still have the manuscript you handed me.

Were still using the cover story of missing persons.
Has been since 2008 with earlier reports covered as hearsay.

TELEGRAPH TOWN

Sparks so bright,
finely cut privet bushes set suburban shapes.

Edges on the narrow margins,
between sanity and forgetting.

Flip the switch to intensity walking
this slip road out of telegraph town.

Speaking of revolution
with changes on hand.

The curse of eviction,
convictions to the letter.

Alighting point only
through telegraph town.

Barterers in value,
frequent appliance in crossed faces.

You scream extremist
in the telegraph merry go round.

IN THE NAME OF MAKING A RECORDING

Garth on Gower in the new Bloomsbury Set,
mid 1990s London hotel dole deal streets.
In for two and a pound for television
with narrow rooms divided by flimsy boards.

One owner, management with volvo and lived elsewhere.

Initially had a breakfast provided in the early months made by
the brother and two sisters whom ran the establishment and lived in.

Other residents residing included
Mr N R my cohort in this story,
a east end painter and decorator named Brian,
Ted the one room socialist surrounded by papers,
a cohabiting musician from the north of the country
whom had a relationship with one of the sisters
as well as the turn over of tourists.

Now winter it was make your own christmas Dickensian breakfast,
having missed the given time slot
our use of the kitchen being observed with strict scrutiny.

Peppered fish with spinach leafs and houmous for lunch or in the evening
with codeine top ups just after. A stable diet for several weeks on end.

Amongst this and skipping some time through several studio visits
in the name of making a recording that never saw the day.

Within the M25 ventured the Toe Rags of the east, valve reaches in the west,
stock pathways up the north, but for some reason never going south.

Saz medicine soon pawned off, but found a high valued postal order
in the street just outside the hotel steps.

Donned the suit and cashed it in.

Weird reality of existence and small survival claims
to help the move on and keep things in line.

Holiday season arrives again, two rooms into one,
tourist moves into my room and I'm next door with Mr N.

The hotel establishment making the extra cash, fleecing the fund,
coincidently Minder being filmed just down the road.

In the end what was wrong
about jamming the knife into the TV box,
recycling the coins and feeding our soul.

Ownership of a liability,
maybe,
but a plan of action was needed to get out.

Pack everything we had into one bag each,
claiming it was a laundry run and never come back.

A week later after holding off any intrusion of room cleaning
as well as the discovery of a small crime.

The plan was put into action and we left the building separately.

THE STEAM DETECTIVES PASSPORT CONTROL

Out of the shadows in
a Brief Encounter 1945 Lean,
silent, but momentary passions in the tea set.

Rattle of the carriage
in a click clack click clack
on the rack, a case rumbles.

Withheld, but boiling over,
plots of meetings through narration
each and every other, weeks on go by.

Pocket watches set, suited and hats doffed,
t-dress, hairpin and floral lines, an arrival awaits shortly.
In the station connection tunnels a love affair ensues
through the steam and smoke, dust and coal brought them here.
Rumbles above, passing and covering,
unsuspected actions running away.

The steam detectives passport control
came into operative function during the conflict of al-sorts,
lines set out in versatile dissection in the stories
of dissidents, re-visionaries and expressionists.

Undercurrents diverting attention in celluloid smoke circles.
A form of manners, inexhaustible plot rationed out in
stamped passes on Brighton Rock 1947 Boulting.

Big bands swing at dances in the Pallas,
fraught jingle jangle on pier steps
as the spivs sway their wares, spliced, spiced and sliced.

Reverse grey coats in the post war
Third Man border control, 1949 Carol Reed intrigue.
Cunning bloody plot, zither,
severing in the underworld and aspiring to the overground.

ODES TO A 1940s FILM SET

The door with seven locks.
Brittle edges, twenty one days all at sea.
Take to the waiting souls in disparate encounters of lost lives.
Regained through surface tales of motion.

A constant dance of red shoes, in matters of life and death.
Pressing turmoils in the corridor of mirrors.
The night has eyes, just east of Piccadilly.
Contraband of the seventh survivor as the saint meets the tiger.

The spider under your hat.
Ghost trains on freedom radio.
Brass monkey, undercover counter-blast.
Tomorrow we live as the balloon goes up.
The day will dawn in an unpublished story.

The agitator swathes in blithe spirit, give me the stars.
The new lot as the night invader, they shout for you alone.
Dreaming men of two worlds, years between the upturned glass.

Vs IN THE WINDOW

It's not so fictional, holding on this thread.
Strengths in the bare cords laid open and in front.
The parts we perform in this ongoing play.
This theatre in knuckle rides looking to the sides in all.

Advance to the board,
Tears of edges, people at source.
Rationing of supply, sustaining the whys.
Question the facts as the rubble is piling.

Syncopated games in conflict aboard this mid-day journey.
Suns are high through the east and west horizons.
In the back talking over each other in co-ordinated chaos.
Conversational variants by land, sea and sky.
The secret payments in order to disrupt the given process.

Orders now projected from valleys afield, proverbial in bright eyes.
The v in the window could be a tick.
Real eyes are now needed in fluctuating appearances.
Headlong into abominable implications through manipulated discourse.
Payed for by the twisted minds, a few gaining on this climate of fear.

Routes in and routing out secrets of those vanished.
Power in the hand, performers in the fields.
Acting on lands, transversing the deep flow.
Whipping up the dust in a quake of murmuring shouts.
Oh, we have not finished it yet!

AND THEN IT COMES BLOWING

In the brief silence on the misted up peak,
movements are at peace and celebrated
through those years now gone.

This next path is now upon us
as the fox travels over the roads,
that morning with scavenged
pickings from the night.

Crows on the wall waiting and watching.
A couple then grab a food packet left
and fly through to the estate, floating in exile.

In these dark days of fake news
and hidden truth we search out
and reach for a closer understanding.

Uncorking the main event in
consciousness of emotion,
a picture resurfaces and its been repackaged
from something once practiced.

No stopping and no surplus to requirements.
Just added the sugar for excreted verbals.

Demolition of this day for that.
Now the high winds are breaking,
baton down the hatches and keep sight.

Exclusion zones now propping up a
universal twist in extreme bullying, a populism of dangers.
Take the word resist and hold that high.

So yes to the forever constant, scavenging
of information for a call out to truth.
Looking out of this commuting glass bubble.

As a women holds that globe upside down.
She's on crutches gripping for the lives of all.
Uncertainty is bound leaning on a fence with an intent stare.

An angular vocal comes out and defeats the monsters.
Supply chains in easy servings to craving.
Bags full in waste glass to the hard place, crawling in terror.

Rummaging with a social conscience.
A bricolage of instrumentation upon spider flight.
Big wheel circles in skeletal expressions.

Jumping the hours, waving the balloons goodbye.
Personalities dream of stamping a path.
Notating the bees at a request in misspelling.

Haircuts today, sofa bound and humanity waiting.
Then shouts from the corner, 'My daughters flat is being flooded'.
Chaos ensues in police being called and cardboard then thrown to the ground.

Radio clock a dial for news in the winds of descent.
Paving stone icons of fortune stars,
but sanctioned isles in paradise streaming.

Broadcasting that everything will be a but.
Hitting the accelerator with no maps or plans.
Treatments of the dots, not filling the blanks.

Braying dogs of contempt, hooting in the aisles.
Laughing at you and so melting the footprint.
Thefts of existence, but rising above with howls in collective control.

White washed roads of deep frustrations.
Co-opera in family assessments.
Grinding the isolated incident to a resource of sounds.

Circulating bullies taking liberties with random strangers.
This crossing of fractions on factional leaning.
A discourse on the micro and macro of mining a soul in belief.

Emerging from the tunnels into a storm of thought.
Observing the microphones and a figure on edge.
Quietly speaking from a balcony of immunity.

Who knows how this may play out in fact.
The twist and strands are rapidly clicking.
Virtues and speeches for all in songs.

Nothing else matters when I hold you in thoughts.
In physical binds my mind out of this box.
Drop uplands in a critical zone.

This heat is on through mass resurgence.
For sale signs flat out and bathing in light.
Slumber of rages temporarily halted in birdsong dawns.

Breathing is steady in this slide by ride.
And when the next phase comes blowing
we take a memory of a face in the throng.

The maps are now being primed and read day to day.
We are just listening out for and waiting
for natures call in those howls of treason.

www.ingramcontent.com/pod-product-compliance
Lightning Source LLC
Chambersburg PA
CBHW070032110426
42741CB00035B/2741